Selected Later Poems of
MARIE LUISE KASCHNITZ

The Lockert Library of Poetry in Translation
Editorial Adviser, John Frederick Nims
For other titles in the Lockert Library, see page 113

Selected
Later Poems of

MARIE LUISE
KASCHNITZ

Translated by
LISEL MUELLER

PRINCETON UNIVERSITY PRESS
PRINCETON, NEW JERSEY

Copyright © 1980 by Princeton University Press

Published by Princeton University Press, Princeton, New Jersey

In the United Kingdom: Princeton University Press, Guildford, Surrey

All Rights Reserved

Library of Congress Cataloging in Publication Data will be found on the last printed page of this book

The Lockert Library of Poetry in Translation is supported by a bequest from Lacy Lockert (1888-1974)

The translator acknowledges assistance by a grant from the Illinois Arts Council, a State agency

This book has been composed in V-I-P Sabon

Clothbound editions of Princeton University Press books are printed on acid-free paper, and binding materials are chosen for strength and durability

Printed in the United States of America by Princeton University Press, Princeton, New Jersey

Contents

Introduction

IT IS STRANGE that the poetry of Marie Luise Kaschnitz (1901-1974) should be introduced to American readers only now. Kaschnitz, who was accorded every possible honor in her native Germany during her lifetime and was invited to read from her work all over the world, was a prodigious writer. Not only did she publish nine collections of poetry; she also wrote more than a dozen volumes of fiction, essays and radio plays, not to mention a biography of Gustave Courbet and several sizable "Journals"—that peculiarly European genre which combines topical observations with broad reflection, autobiography, and fiction. Her publisher is currently in the process of issuing her complete works in eight volumes. The first two, numbering around two thousand pages, have already appeared.

Kaschnitz began to write at an early age, yet I think of her as a late bloomer, in the sense that her subtlest and most memorable work was written in the last two decades of her life. Nor was there any diminution of her creative energy in the period immediately preceding her death; her final collection of poetry and two volumes of essays appeared during the last three years of her life, when she was in her early seventies. I suspect the reasons for this late fullness are both historical and personal. For writers who remained in Germany during the Nazi regime, the tyranny and enforced cultural isolation, and later the disasters of war with their aftermath, including the spiritual reckoning, must have been an enormous deterrent to artistic development, when it did not drive them into complete silence. Additionally, her strengths as a writer do not lie so much in the overflow of lyrical imagination that we associate with youth, as in the articulation of the slow, painful self-discoveries that come with time and suffering.

Her life falls into three distinct phases. The first began with her childhood on the estate of her aristocratic family, near Karlsruhe, which she abandoned as a young woman in order to support herself. In 1925 she married Guido Kaschnitz von Weinberg, an archeologist. The marriage seems to have been exceptionally close, and she accompanied her husband on all his travels to Rome, Sicily, and other ancient sites in the Mediterranean. These travels generated some poetry and a great deal of prose, in which the sense of place is extremely important. The second phase began in the 1940s, when she and her husband and daughter found themselves among the living after the firebombings of Frankfurt, where she lived most of her life, a city filled with the dead and those who, like herself, were "merely" homeless. The third was her life without her husband, who died during the 1950s after a painful illness. His death was devastating for her. To judge from her journals and poems, as well as from biographical sources (though she was very reticent), she virtually withdrew from active life for several years, and it took extraordinary effort for her to survive as a human being and a writer, and to return eventually from her isolation.

Each of these acts of survival initiated its particular kind of poetry. After the war she and most other German writers thought of themselves as voices of conscience, voices that had the responsibility of dealing with guilt and suffering. She wanted to speak for the dead and the martyred, and to help heal the survivors. She did not want her countrymen to forget.

It is impossible to understand the poets of Kaschnitz's generation outside of their historical context. The history of Germany from 1914 until the 1950s is one extended nightmare; no individual life remained untouched by it. There can have been few times in history when personal life was so inextricably bound up with public events. Bertolt Brecht wrote of the fate of emigrés who, like himself, were forced to "change countries more often than shoes." Those writers who stayed in Germany were witnesses to, and victims of, the unprecedented catastrophe of the Second World War. There was no way for these writers and those of the next generation to write except in the context of that catastrophe and the evil which led to it; they had to be "engaged." What is more, they had to make connections. They could not ignore the postwar nuclear arms race and the cold war (with Germany at its political and geographical center), which continually threatened to become a hot one. They could not ignore the complacency of the German public, its willingness to forget, any more than they could ignore the rapid advance of technology with its danger to human values. Some, like Günter Eich, despaired. Marie Luise Kaschnitz continued to speak out. She believed in speech as exorcism, and she once said she wanted to think of herself as a "watchman," a role she adopted when she recognized with horror that her silence during the Nazi period meant de facto complicity, no matter how great her private loathing. (In a poem included here, "Ein Aufhebens machen" ["Making a Fuss"], she discusses the thanklessness of the "watchman's" role and the trauma of having to relive agonizing experiences.)

The voice in the poems of the postwar years, then, was elegiac, exhortative, prophetic, public. But after a book-length poem about Rome, *Ewige Stadt (Eternal City)*, which can be thought of as intermediate in style and tone, *Neue Gedichte (New Poems)* appeared in 1957. The poems in this collection break with her earlier mode. Though she does not abdicate her responsibility to "look out" for the rest of us, she also dares to speak about herself, her own life, which at this time involved deeply felt Mediterranean impressions. Many of these poems are about places; they attempt to equate feeling with location. In subsequent volumes, landscape remains important and often emblematic, but it becomes internalized and the identification of specific places diminishes.

Dein Schweigen—meine Stimme (Your Silence—My Voice), her next collection of poems (1962), has at its center her husband's death and deals touchingly with her divided self, whose life-affirming half keeps surprising the other, defeated, one. In the present selection I have included only one of numerous poems which deal specifically with her loss, but all the poems included are obviously written against the background of that loss; it is the basic assumption from which they proceed.

The pull of opposing forces, here represented by the conflict between her longing for death and her native liveliness and curiosity, became characteristic of her poetry. It provides the tension that underlies the last two collections as well. In these, *Ein Wort weiter (One Word Further)* and *Kein Zauberspruch (No Magic Formula)*, published in 1965 and 1972 and preoccupied with old age and approaching death, she is continually wrestling with dualities. She longs for transcendence, yet she is passionately attached to common reality. She recognizes the ephemeral nature of human consciousness in the universe, yet her poems are celebrations of it. She needs the sense of permanence given her by places like Sicily, where modern history has hardly affected tradition, yet she welcomes the new, if not without trepidation. She sets alongside a poem that proclaims her readiness to die one that asserts her undiminished participation in, even appetite for, the full life. It is no wonder that Rome, with its blend of the temporal and eternal, remained her favorite city. She died there in 1974; no doubt it was her wish.

Neue Gedichte marks a break in more than one respect. Not only does Kaschnitz move from a public to a personal voice, she also abandons rhymed, metrical verse. For the first time she writes poems in the short, elliptical lines that make her late work unmistakable. Essentially she manages two distinct stylistic modes: the proselike syntax and long lines reserved for her narrative poems ("Hiroshima" and "Uralt" ["Ancient"], for example) and the sparse, abrupt, heavily accented and unpunctuated manner of her lyrics. She had said, when she accepted the Georg Büchner Prize in 1955, that she wanted to express the hardest, most painful, inner reality, and she seems to have found a garment for it: of plain cloth, unembroidered and close-fitting.

The shift to more private speech strikes me as important. The switch from "we" to "I" allowed the poet and her persona to come together, as they had not done before, and to free a lyrical voice that was uniquely hers. Yet there was never any danger of solipsism. She never wavered in her belief that writers must bear witness, nor abandoned her defense of objective values. "Affection is still affection, overcoming is still overcoming, betrayal is still betrayal," she said in an interview. She could not be less than passionately committed to the world, including its absurdities, as long as she lived. It is precisely the interaction of the lyrical self of a woman trying to come to terms with death, and the world with its data banks and opera houses "with white concrete sails," that makes her last volume so moving. She sees no reason for optimism, but carries "the paper pennant of confidence" nonetheless. Her tragic sense was balanced by her belief in human viability; she is after all proof of it. Above all she is a poet of continuities, the continuity of nature and the continuity of history, that is, human consciousness. The loss of demarcations between places and periods of time, which occurs in old age, served her well as a metaphor in her last collection.

The selection presented here contains work from Kaschnitz's last four books of poetry. In omitting her earlier work, I have assumed the translator/editor's prerogative of choosing what I considered strongest, as well as presenting that part of her poetry which I believe to be of greatest interest to present-day American readers. My selection ignores her longer, sequential poems in favor of her short ones, and by doing so, deemphasizes the elegiac and meditative voice. Finally, translatability helped to determine the choice of poems. My experience in rendering German poetry into English has convinced me that those poets who, like Rilke, exploit the conceptual possibilities of the German language through syntactical means, are those most resistant to translation. Trakl's reputation in this country, which is disproportionate to the modest body of work he was able to produce before his early death, is the result of his translatability. In her later work, Kaschnitz, like Trakl, excels in the hard-edged phrase and the visual, even pictorial, image; elements which are particularly conducive to the English language and the modern sensibility.

Having chosen poems that lend themselves to American English has enabled me to translate with considerable faithfulness. Faithfulness is not synonymous with literalness, of course. I have tried to translate closely whenever it was possible and consistent with my aim of rendering English versions that could stand as poems. But faithfulness to Kaschnitz's rigorous tone sometimes forced me to depart from literally translating colloquial and formulaic phrases that would be puzzling in English; instead, I sought cultural or idiomatic equivalents. Also, I sometimes found it necessary to change the deliberately scrambled syntax for the sake of clarity, all the more because the reader gets no help from Kaschnitz's punctuation, which is sparse or nonexistent. German, a highly inflected language, permits enormous flexibility of word order, and therefore emphasis, without sacrificing intelligibility, while in English word order of a sentence determines its meaning. My decision to "straighten out" Kaschnitz's syntax at times makes it seem more conventional than it is. I regret this, but see no way out. To have rendered these poems as syntactically obscure structures in English would have been a greater violation.

From
NEUE GEDICHTE
(1957)

Hiroshima

Der den Tod auf Hiroshima warf
Ging ins Kloster, läutet dort die Glocken.
Der den Tod auf Hiroshima warf
Sprang vom Stuhl in die Schlinge, erwürgte sich.
Der den Tod auf Hiroshima warf
Fiel in Wahnsinn, wehrt Gespenster ab
Hunderttausend, die ihn angehen nächtlich
Auferstandene aus Staub für ihn.

Nichts von alledem ist wahr.
Erst vor kurzem sah ich ihn
Im Garten seines Hauses vor der Stadt.
Die Hecken waren noch jung und die Rosenbüsche zierlich.
Das wächst nicht so schnell, daß sich einer verbergen könnte
Im Wald des Vergessens. Gut zu sehen war
Das nackte Vorstadthaus, die junge Frau
Die neben ihm stand im Blumenkleid
Das kleine Mädchen an ihrer Hand
Der Knabe der auf seinem Rücken saß
Und über seinem Kopf die Peitsche schwang.
Sehr gut erkennbar war er selbst
Vierbeinig auf dem Grasplatz, das Gesicht
Verzerrt von Lachen, weil der Photograph
Hinter der Hecke stand, das Auge der Welt.

Hiroshima

The man who dropped death on Hiroshima
Has taken vows, rings the bells in the cloister.
The man who dropped death on Hiroshima
Jumped into a noose and hanged himself.
The man who dropped death on Hiroshima
Has gone insane, fights apparitions
Made out of dust that come for him,
Hundreds of thousands every night.

None of all this is true.
Just the other day I saw him
In his front yard in the suburbs.
The hedges were low and the rosebushes dainty.
It takes time to raise an oblivious forest
For someone to hide in. Plain to see
The new, naked house, the young wife
Beside him in her flowered dress
The little girl holding her hand
The boy who was sitting across his back
Cracking a whip over his head.
He himself was easy to recognize
On all fours on his lawn, his face
A grimace of laughter, because the photographer stood
Outside the hedge, the eye of the world.

Karte von Sizilien

Ich zeichne Euch den Umriß. Einen Flügel
Wie von der Schulter einer Siegesgöttin.
Den Aufriß, eine Scholle Felsgebirge
Stehen geblieben unterm Glanz der Sonne
Indes mit Tang und Sand und Zug der Fische
Das Meer die süßen Ebenen bedeckt.
Das dunkle Strichwerk meint den Sturz der Hänge.
Flußtäler sieben bleiben ausgespart.
Ein Zackenkranz der Berg, wo Eis und Feuer
Heilige Hochzeit halten. Jetzt rückt näher
Am Abendtisch. Den Ölkrug heb ich auf.
Wo ich die Tropfen fallen lasse, wachsen
Wälder von schwarz und silbernen Oliven.
Wo ich das Brot zerkrümle, weht die Saat
Auf roten Hügeln, weiter Weg der Pflugschar.
Das weiße Salz im Osten ausgeschüttet
Meint Nahrung aus dem Meere, Salz und Fische
Aber das gelbe Mondviertel Citrone im Norden
Schatten der Laubendächer. Süßen Blühduft.
Die roten Pfeile, ausgestreckt im Meer
Dieser vom Festland, dieser von Afrika,
Dieser von Spanien, der aus der Peloponnes
Sind die Schiffswege der fremden Eroberer.
Nun hebt vom Gartenpfad die weißen Kiesel
Zu zweien, dreien. Glänzen sie Euch nicht
Tempeln und Domen gleich im Mondeslicht—
Doch stampf ich mit den Füßen, seht
Wie sie schüttern und tanzen
Wie im Beben der Erde der fällt, der steht.
Die Lampe rück ich fort und wieder her
Und wieder fort. Nun Licht. Nun Dunkelheit.
Glanz und Verderben, ewiger Widerstreit.

A Map of Sicily

I'll draw the outline for you. It's a wing
From the shoulder of a victory goddess.
The side view is a chunk of rugged mountain
Arrested in the brightness of the sun,
The sea around it covering the plain
With sand and seaweed and with schools of fish.
Striated lines are for steep elevations.
The seven river valleys are left blank.
The toothed crown means the mountain where the wedding
Of fire and ice takes place. Move in a little
Around the table. Look, I tip the oil jug.
Wherever you see drops fall on the table
Is where the black and silver olives grow.
Wherever I drop breadcrumbs, think of crops
On the red hills, the wide range of the plowshares.
The salt I pour, this whiteness in the east,
Stands for food from the ocean, salt and fish;
The lemon wedge, a piece of the yellow moon,
For shade of arbors, sweetly scented flowers.
I'll draw red arrows clear across the ocean,
One from the mainland, one from Africa,
One from Peloponnesus, one from Spain,
To show you the routes of foreign conquerors.
Now run out to the garden path and bring
Some small white pebbles. Don't they look to you
Like cupolas and temples in the moonlight—
But watch, I'll stamp my feet
And they shake and dance;
Nothing can keep from falling in an earthquake.
I'll pull the lamp forward and push it back,
Pull it forward again. Now light. Now darkness.
Splendor and death, eternal argument.

5

Wo ist der kleine Bauer, den ich mir
Aus Brot geknetet? Dieser steht noch immer
Die Hacke in der Hand. Ein wenig tiefer
Gebeugt als zu Beginn. Was ist das Ganze?
Brot, Blut und Stein. Ein Stückchen Abendland.

Where is the little peasant that I kneaded
Out of a piece of bread? Still there, as always
Hands on his hoe. Bent down a little more
Than at the start. And now, what is all this?
Bread, blood and stone. A piece of the Western world.

Segesta

In der Hand das Gefühl von winzigen Schneckenhäusern
Zwergpalmenschäften und Dornen der Aloe.
Unterm Fuße Geröll und uralten Pflasterstein.
Im Ohr das Angstgeschrei der kleinen Vögel
Der Bewohner der Schlucht, der aufgescheuchten
Vom Flügelschlag des Räubers.

Regen, Regen
Auf dem Dach der hilflosen Hütte.
Gespräch der Eingeschlossenen von alter Sorge
Uralter Krankheit Armut.

Am Nachmittag der helle Streifen Blau
Im Westen. Fortgeschoben Zoll
Um Zoll die schwere Decke. Irisfeuer
In jedem Tropfen. Macchiagesumm.

Maultiergespanne wachsen aus dem Acker
Pflüge der Vorzeit. Einsame Eselreiter
Schwarze, erscheinen wieder am Saume des Himmels.

Die Abendsonne saugt ertrunkene
Gehöfte aus dem Schlamm und Fensterscheiben
Mit kleinem rotem Licht darin zu glühen.

Vögel reißen empor die verkrusteten Wälder.
Schmetterlinge rasten auf Kohlgerippen
Auf den eisernen Sternen der Artischocke.

Tief in die Nacht, die andre Verlassenheit
Leuchtet der namenlose
Unvergängliche Tempel.
Säule und Schwelle
Und die erhabene Stirn.

Segesta

Hands feel the contours of minute snail shells
Trunks of dwarf palm and thorns of aloe.
Feet walk on rubble and ancient pavement.
Ears catch the panic of small birds
Ravine-dwellers, scared up
By a predator's wingbeat.

Rain, rain
On the roof of the helpless shack.
The shut-ins talk of old worries
Poverty, the ancient disease.

In the afternoon a bright streak of blue
In the west. The heavy blanket is pushed
Back inch by inch. Iris on fire
In every drop. The *macchia* hums.

Mule teams spring up on the land
Primeval plows. Lone riders on donkeys
Reappear, black, at the rim of the sky.

The evening sun sucks drowned
Farms from the mud and glows
In their windows with a small red light.

Birds upright the encrusted woods.
Moths rest on cabbage skeletons
And on artichokes, iron stars.

Late into the night, another loneliness
Shines, the nameless
Eternal temple:
Doorway and columns
And the majestic façade.

9

Selinunt

Was sie vom Krieg erzählen, von den Tausend
Zerstörten Städten, überrascht mich nicht.
Gott hat die sechzig Säulen des Tempels C
Auf einmal umgeworfen. Er hat dazu
Keine Bomben und keine schweren Geschütze gebraucht
Nur einen einzigen tieferen Atemzug.

Fremde kommen, wenn die Mandelwälder
Blühen, viele über den Hügel.
Die Sonne blitzt in ihren Windschutzscheiben.
Nicht nach Schafwolle riechen sie, nicht nach Erde
Ihre Kleider fühlen sich an wie gesponnenes Glas.
Keiner weiß, wie das ist, wenn der Abend kommt
Wenn die letzten Scheinwerfer hinter den Bergen verschwinden
Wie dann die einsamen Hunde bellen landüber
Wie unter den Sternen die Grillen schreien.

Mein kleiner Bruder hüpft im hölzernen Ställchen.
Die roten Lilien auf der Wachstuchdecke
Tanzen im Schimmer der Petroleumlampe.
Mein Vater sucht den schwangeren Schoß
Meiner gelben, verwelkten Mutter
An die verbrannte Küste schlägt das Meer.

Wenn mein Bräutigam ruft, der Lammträger, zittere ich.
Wasser gehen wir holen vom Brunnen der Totengöttin
Er preßt seinen Mund auf meinen Mund.
Niemals werd ich die gläsernen Nachtstädte sehen
Sagt die Tochter des Wächters von Selinunt.

Selinunte

What they tell of the war, about thousands
Of cities destroyed, doesn't surprise me.
God blew down the sixty pillars
Of Temple C all at once. He needed
Neither bombs nor heavy artillery
Only a single breath.

When the almond groves flower
Strangers come over the hill.
The sun glints in their windshields.
They don't smell of sheep's-wool and earth
Their clothes feel like spun glass.
They don't know what it's like after dark
When the last headlights have slid down the mountains
How the lone dogs bark in the distance
How the cicadas scream under the stars.

My little brother plays in the woodshed.
Red lilies dance on the oilcloth
In the light of the kerosene lamp.
My father embraces the pregnant body
Of my drained, faded mother.
The ocean beats on the scorched coast.

When my sweetheart the shepherd calls me, I tremble.
We go to the spring of the goddess of death for water
He presses his mouth against my mouth.
I'll never see the night cities of glass
Says the watchman's daughter of Selinunte.

Hic jacet Pirandello

Ausbedungen hatte sich der Dichter
Ein anderes Grab. Ein luftigeres.
Leichenbegängnis bei Nacht im Armensarg
Gebein im Feuer und die Handvoll Asche
Vom Wind ergriffen, dem der gerade weht.

Heimgeholt wider seinen Willen hat man ihn
Urne zu Urne. Tönernes Gefäß
Zu tönernem Gefäß. Wo flüchtige
Mädchen der Quellgründe tanzen und fette Silene
Gefangene hinter dem staubigen Glas.

Welch eine Ruhstatt für den Ruhelosen
Die suchenden Füße
Die Brauen, die zuckten
Den Mund, der formte Tag und Nacht
Die finstere Sage der Armen.

Wie kann dem Wandernden behagen, hier
Umgang zu halten mit den lüsternen
Kustoden und den ausgesetzten Fremden?
Kein Schrei, kein Duft
Kein Strahl des Mittagslichts—

Tritt näher, sieh bei schon vergilbtem Buch
Die bauchige Amphore. Grund so schwarz
Wie Lavastein Siziliens, roter Schmelzfluß
Wie Weizenerde Agrigents.
Und Helena, die lieblichste, behütend
Das zerfallene Herz des Dichters.

Hic Jacet Pirandello

The poet stipulated
A different grave. An airier one.
A pauper's funeral in the night
A secret fire and the handful of ashes
Seized by the wind, whichever wind was blowing.

Against his will he was brought home
Urn to urn, clay container
To clay container. Here, where elusive
Naiads dance with fat satyrs
Caught behind dusty glass.

What a resting place for the restless man
The searching feet
Twitching eyebrows
The lips perpetually shaping
The dark legend of the poor.

How can the wanderer bear to be
On familiar terms with the lewd
Custodians and the alien displays?
No sound, no scent
No ray from the noon sun—

Look closer: next to the yellowed book
A bulging amphora. Background black
As Sicilian lava rock, a river
Red as the wheatland of Agrigento.
And Helen, the loveliest, guarding
The poet's ruined heart.

Der Eingeweihte

Aus dem Tambourin hat er gegessen
Aus der Zymbel hat er getrunken
Ein

Knabe hockend im Reisfeld
Furcht mit dem Finger
Die schwarze Erde
Ein

Knabe springt über
Gespiegelte Wolken
Hierhin dorthin
Unter den Wolken
Ein

Knabe hebt seine
Stimme und Schwärme
Von Worten gehen
Wie Vogelzüge
Aus seiner Brust.

Irgendwo inmitten
Der brüllenden Städte
Ich
Senke das Antlitz
Schreibe.

The Initiate

He has eaten from the tambourine
He has drunk from the cymbal
A

Boy crouched in a rice field
Plows the black earth
With one finger
A

Boy leaps over
Reflected clouds
This way and that way
Under the clouds
A

Boy lifts his
Voice and flocks
Of words arise
Like bird formations
From his throat

Somewhere amidst
The hubbub of cities
I
Lower my face
And write.

Bräutigam Froschkönig

Wie häßlich ist
Dein Bräutigam
Jungfrau Leben

Eine Rüsselmaske sein Antlitz
Eine Patronentasche sein Gürtel
Ein Flammenwerfer
Seine Hand

Dein Bräutigam Froschkönig
Fährt mit Dir
(Ein Rad fliegt hierhin, eins dorthin)
Über die Häuser der Toten

Zwischen zwei
Weltuntergängen
Preßt er sich
In Deinen Schoß

Im Dunkeln nur
Ertastest Du
Sein feuchtes Haar

Im Morgengrauen
Nur im
Morgengrauen
Nur im

Erblickst Du seine
Traurigen
Schönen
Augen.

The Frog Prince Bridegroom

How ugly he is
Your bridegroom
Mistress Life

With a gas mask for a face
A cartridge belt for hips
A flame thrower for a hand

Your bridegroom the frog prince flies with you
(Wheels spinning in all directions)
Over the houses of the dead

Between Doomsday
And Doomsday
He eases himself
Into your body

In the darkness
All you touch is
His damp hair

Only when it dawns
Only when
It dawns
Only when

Do you discover his
Sad
Beautiful
Eyes.

Erwartung

Am Abend wenn die
Kinder unter Palmen
Frage und Antwort singen und
Das Glöckchen läutet

Noch nicht Zeit
Entgegenzugehen
Den kleinen Stadtschritt
Entgegen dem Zug
Der durch Fiebersümpfe
Im roten Schräglicht
Nicht Zeit

Für das Herzklopfen unter
Der Lautsprecherstimme
Für die raschen stoßweisen
Wortes des Willkomms.

Nur diese
Langsam heran
Wachsende Gegenwart
Diese sich unaufhaltsam
Ausbreitende Landschaft Liebe
Felder voll Schwertgras und Rose
Lebendiges Wasser
Wind.

Expectancy

In the evening when the
Children under the palm trees
Sing questions and answers and
The little bell rings

Not yet time
To set out to meet you
Take the short walk into town
To meet the train
On its way through the fever swamps
By red slanting light
Not time

For the heart to pound
Under the loudspeaker's voice
For the quick breathless
Words of welcome

Only this
Slowly
Expanding presence
This inexorably
Growing landscape of love
Fields filled with grasses and roses
Living water
A wind.

Liebe Sonne

Wir glauben an diese
Unsere große
Freiheit zu sterben
Häuser unsere
Einstürzen zu lassen
Weingärten unsere
Brach—

Wir glauben es zwänge
Uns niemand aufzuerstehen
Späterhin in das Licht
In die gewaltige
Anstrengung ewigen Lebens.

Wir glauben es stünde bei uns
Niemanden mehr zu lieben
Und hintreiben zu lassen endlich
Erkaltet in kalten Schwärmen
Diesen unseren Stern.

Aber die unverminderte
Tägliche Zeugenschaft
Küssender Lippen
Liebe Sonne
Schöne Erde
Ewig ewig
Weiß es besser.

Dear Sun

We believe in it
Our great
Freedom to die
Allow our houses
To collapse
Our vineyards to lie
Fallow—

We believe no one can force us
Ever again to rise
From death into the light
Into the enormous
Effort of the afterlife.

We believe the time has come
To stop loving anyone
And give up our planet
Let it drift
Cold among cold satellites.

But the undiminished
Daily witness
Of lips kissing
Dear sun
Good earth
Forever and ever
Knows better.

Picasso in Rom

Zertrümmertes Antlitz des Menschen
Löwen und Wolfsgesicht
Auftauchend inmitten
Und blutiger Halbmond.

Ein Auge belauernd
Das andere
Zwischen gespaltener
Wange und Wange
Hervorgetrieben
Die Eiterbeule.

Kinder strotzen im
Bleichen gierigen
Fettfleisch. Dachüber
Schleicht die dämonische
Katze. Zerissenen
Vogel im Zahn.

Und draußen um
Die zuckergußweiße
Säulenhalle

Die wundgefetze
Von brüllenden Fahrgeschossen
Die leidende
Klarheit
Abend.

Picasso in Rome

The human face is smashed
Faces of lions and wolves
Amidst the pieces
And a bloody half-moon.

One eye spies on
The other.
Between cleft
Cheek and cheek
A festering boil
Bulges.

Children strut in their
Pale greedy
Bloated flesh. A demonic
Cat slinks across
The roofs. A torn
Bird in its teeth.

And outside, surrounding
The white icing
Of the columned hall

Lacerated
In the gunfire of engines
That wounded
Clarity
Evening.

From
DEIN SCHWEIGEN—
MEINE STIMME
(1962)

Schrecklicher noch

Deine Ferne ist ungeheuer
(Wir hörten so
Von Sternennebeln die fliehen)
Aber schrecklicher deine Nähe
Deine heimliche Gegenwart
Deine Schritte
Dein Atem
Deine geflüsterten Worte
Dein Schrei um Hilfe.

More Terrible

Your distance is immense
(We have heard something
About galaxies fleeing)
But far more terrible is your nearness
Your secret presence
Your footsteps
Your breath
Your whispered words
Your cry for help.

Schreibend

Schreibend wollte ich
Meine Seele retten.
Ich versuchte Verse zu machen
Es ging nicht.
Ich versuchte Geschichten zu erzählen
Es ging nicht.
Man kann nicht schreiben
Um seine Seele zu retten.
Die aufgegebene treibt dahin und singt.

By Writing

By writing I wanted
To save my soul.
I tried to make poems
It did not work.
I tried to tell stories
It did not work.
You cannot write
To save your soul.
Given up, it drifts and does the singing.

Anders

Will sich nicht mehr behaupten
Armes Haupt.
Fällt in den Nacken
Zählt das Schilf am Himmel
Und die Fischerlichter die Sterne.
Sinkt auf die Brust
Da ticken die Warnsignale
Eine bündige Sprache.

Wer endete seine Musik
Noch mit vollem Akkord
Oder gar mit Posaunen?

Wir haben gesungen
Die Katze hat uns geholt.
Jetzt singen wir wieder
Sagen noch manchmal
Du Meer
Du Liebe
Aber anders
Mit kleinerem Atem.

Differently

Refuses to be headstrong
Poor head
Falls backwards face up
Counts the reeds in the sky
And the trolling lights, the stars
Drops on your chest
With its warning signals
A no-nonsense language

Who ends his music
With a full chord these days
Not to speak of trombones?

We used to sing
Cat got our tongues
Now we are singing again
Sometimes we still
Say ocean
Say love
But differently
With shorter breath.

Lebensbaum

Der Lindenbaum
Lebensbaum schreit
In der Blätterfallnacht
Sein grelles Kiwitt
Sein Kindweintimschlaf.

Dreht euch nicht um
Legt die Hände aufs Haar
Lehnt die Stirn
An die Bettlakenmauer.

Draußen der Plünderer Wind
Reißt die Goldparmänen ins Wildgras
Um Quitte und Dornengebüsch
Brandet ein salziger Tau.

Im Gezweige die Toten
Die kleingesichtigen
Cherubim
Kreuzen die Flügel voll Pfauenaugen
Hüpfen astaufwärts.

Blattraum Herzraum
Auch wir
Ehe wir schlafen
Bedecken die Landschaft mit Küssen.

Tree of Life

In the night of the falling leaves
The linden
Tree of life screams
A bird's shrill screech
A child's cry in his sleep.

Don't turn around
Put your hands on your heads
Face the wall of your bedsheets

A looter of a wind
Is yanking the golden apples into the grass
A salty dew washes
Around the quince and the brambles.

In the branches, death
Cherubim
With small faces
Cross their iridescent wings
Hop higher up in the trees

Leaf space, heart space
Before we sleep
We too
Cover the landscape with kisses.

Interview

Wenn er kommt, der Besucher,
Der Neugierige und dich fragt,
Dann bekenne ihm, daß du keine Briefmarken sammelst,
Keine farbigen Aufnahmen machst,
Keine Kakteen züchtest.
Daß du kein Haus hast,
Keinen Fernsehapparat,
Keine Zimmerlinde.
Daß du nicht weißt,
Warum du dich hinsetzt und schreibst,
Unwillig, weil es dir kein Vergnügen macht.
Daß du den Sinn deines Lebens immer noch nicht
Herausgefunden hast, obwohl du schon alt bist.
Daß du geliebt hast, aber unzureichend,
Daß du gekämpft hast, aber mit zaghaften Armen.
Daß du an vielen Orten zuhause warst,
Aber ein Heimatrecht hast an keinem.
Daß du dich nach dem Tode sehnst und ihn fürchtest.
Daß du kein Beispiel geben kannst als dieses:
Immer noch offen.

Interview

When the visitor comes,
Prying, questioning you,
Confess that you collect no stamps,
Take no color photographs,
Raise no cacti.
That you own no house,
No television set,
No room-sized fig tree.
That you do not know
Why you sit down and write,
Grudgingly, since it gives you no pleasure.
That you still have not found the meaning
Of your life, although you are getting old.
That you have loved, but not enough,
That you have fought back, but timidly.
That you have lived in many places,
But can call none of them your home.
That you want to die and are afraid.
That you can set no example except this:
Still open.

Uralt

Meines Verwandten eines Aug ist tot,
Das andre, schon geschrumpft, beginnt zu sterben.
Er trägt seine Tränen in Säcken unter den Lidern
Und schreibt seinen Vers in die Luft mit brandigem Zeh.
Alles, was um ihn geschieht, vergißt er sofort,
Aber der alte Bettlerpfad Erinnerung
Führt ihn weiter und weiter und seine Gefährten
Totfreund und Totfrau reden deutlicher alle Tage.
Nach seinem schönsten Erlebnis befragt,
Nennt er nicht seine Hochzeit, auch nicht seine Heimkehr vom
    Kriege,
Sondern einen Sternschnuppenfall, einen gewaltigen,
An den sich niemand erinnert.
Er füttert die Vögel nicht mehr auf dem Winterbrett,
Nur der struppigen Amsel, dem verwundeten Wildling,
Hält er seinen Finger zum Hacken hin,
Starrt sie an mit wächsernen Augen.
Er träumt davon,
Im Herbst in den Wald zu gehen, kurz vor dem ersten Schneefall
Und nicht mehr nachhause zu kommen.
Er träumt vom Laub,
Das ihn bedeckt und vom Gras, das sein Becken umkleidet,
Wenn die Eichelhäher zu seinen Häupten schreien.
Aber er wird im Bett sterben wie alle.
Man wird ihm die Hände falten und sagen, daß es Zeit für ihn
    war,
Daß er alles gehabt hat, was einer verlangen kann,
Und ein gesegnetes Alter.

Ancient

My relative has one dead eye,
The other, already shrunken, has started dying.
He carries his tears in pouches under his lids
And writes a poem in the air with a gangrenous toe.
Whatever happens around him, he forgets it at once,
But the old beggar's route of memory
Leads him on and on, and his companions
Deadfriend and Deadwife make more and more sense.
Asked about his most cherished experience,
He names neither his wedding nor his return from the war,
But a meteor shower, a tremendous one,
Which no one remembers at all.
He has stopped feeding the birds at the windowsill
But offers a finger to a scraggly
Blackbird, a wounded wildling, to peck,
Staring at it with waxen eyes.
He is dreaming of going
Into the woods in autumn, shortly before the first snow,
And not to come home again.
He is dreaming of leaves
That cover him and of grass clothing his body
As jays scream overhead.
But he will die in bed like everyone else.
They will fold his hands and say it was time,
That his life was all he could have asked for
And his old age a godsend.

Ein Aufhebens machen

Schlaf überkommt den Schlaf
Hochzeiter Traum
Leichtfüßig unterwegs
Mit silbernen goldenen Mandeln
Tritt auf der Stelle.
Der Vogel Nachtwald fliegt davon
Und schweigt.
Der Narr bedeckt
Mit seiner Hand die Schellen.

Heb deine Gerte
Schwarzgeflügelte
Seele des Toten
Reisekamerad.
Zerreiß das Schleierspiel
Auf meiner Netzhaut
Aus der Brandung schrei
Mir Möwe das Rätselwort zu.

Denn ein Fischer bin ich zu alt
Den Fisch an die Bootswand zu schlagen
Aber die Wetterbank schwarze
Seh ich im Westen.

Ein Jäger bin ich zu alt
Nicht zu zittern beim Blattschuß
Aber ich unterscheide
Die Tritte von Lämmern und Wölfen.

Wenn ich vorlesen soll
Verschwinden die Blätter
Mir unter den Händen.
Auswendig weiß ich das Dunkle.

Making a Fuss

Sleep overcomes the sleep
Of newlyweds   A dream
With silver and gold almonds
Moving about light-footed
Is running in place.
The bird called nightwood flies away
Is silent.
The fool covers
The bells with his hand.

Lift your wand
Black-winged
Soul of my dead
Traveling companion.
Tear down the cryptic
Charade on my retina
Scream out the secret
O gull from the breakers.

I am too old a fisherman
To dash a fish against the boat
But I can recognize a black
Cloud bank in the west.

Too old a hunter to take aim
Steadily at a shoulder blade
But I can tell the tracks
Of lambs and wolves apart.

When I read from my work
The pages vanish
Between my hands.
I have the dark part memorized.

Ich frage wem dringt das Gerücht
Von der Endzeit unter die Haut?
Wer verläßt sein Haus
Setzt sich unter den wilden Birnbaum?
Wer legt seine Kleider ans Ufer
Und wandert herzeinwärts?

Die das Nachsehen haben
Nachsehen den Flüssen der Sonne
Den enteilenden Schritten
Ach die Erde ist ihnen noch zugetan
Und die brennende Weide.
Die Granittrommel schlägt ihnen Mut zu
Der Regen richtet sie auf.

Mich und meine Brüder
Die todesmutig
Ein Amt übernehmen
Dem niemand gewachsen ist.

Mich und meine Brüder
Die Ausgesetzten im Fellkleid
Die alles noch einmal ersinnen
Auf der Insel Verzweiflung.

Was wir dir sagten
Erde einst
Unsern Lobspruch
Auf dein Schilf deinen Staub deine Rosen
Trägst du uns wieder zu
Gespenstiges Echo.

I ask whose skin is crawling
At the rumor of time running out?
Who abandons his home
And settles under the wild pear tree?
Who leaves his clothes on the shore
And walks in the direction of the heart?

Those who have the lookout
Look out for rivers for the sun
For departing footsteps
O the earth and its burning willows
Still reach out to them.
Granite drums up courage
And rain refreshes them.

Myself and my brothers
Courting death
We are not equal
To what we take on.

Myself and my brothers
In animal skins
Left on the island of despair
Where we invent it all once more.

Earth what we said
What we used to tell you
Our hymn of praise
To your seeds your dust your roses
Returns as an echo
Comes back to haunt us.

Einen Nachglanz hab ich im Auge
Von Seestädten
Bräuten des Meeres.
Von finsterblauem Gewölk
Überfliegend das Maisfeld.

Immer noch will ich
Ein Aufhebens machen
Vom Tod von der Liebe.
Und auf den geäderten
Marmor des Tisches
Ins Weiße Euch schreiben
Abendrotzeit.

An afterimage remains
Of ocean cities
Brides of the sea
Of blue-black clouds
Flying over a cornfield.

I will go on
Making a fuss
About death about love.
And write it down
On your veined marble table
Scratch it into the white
That the sun sets red.

Ich und Ich

Mein Ich und Ich
Eines steht aufrecht
Faßt noch ins Auge
Greift noch die Handvoll
Spürt noch den Hundsschweiß
Den Winterbiß

Eines schon lange
Zur Wande gekehrt
Liest auf dem Mörtel
Die Flugschrift der Träume
Sieht ein durchscheinendes
Wandernd ein Licht.

Ich sagt zu Ich
Harre aus.
Ich fragt Ich
Wem zuliebe?
Ich sagt zu Ich
Bring zu Ende.
Ich fragt Ich
Warum?

Ich der Fisch
Ich die Reuse
Ich der Apfel
Ich das Messer
Ich das Maiskorn
Ich die Henne

Ich der Faden
Ich die Nadel.
Ich die Nadel fängt den Faden
Zieht den roten
Kettenstich.

I and I

I and I:
One still upright
Still looking closely
Still getting its own
Still feels the dog days
The bite of winter.

The other already
Turned to the wall
Nursing what dreams
Appear in the plaster
What ephemeral
Light comes through.

I tells I
Endure.
I asks I
Who cares?
I tells I
Time to stop.
I asks I
What for?

I the fish
I the net
I the apple
I the knife
I the kernel of corn
I the hen
I the thread
I the needle.
I the needle catches the thread
Draws up the red
Chain stitch.

Gegen Abend

Eine kleine Wendung, noch eine
Und du stehst gegen Abend.
Mit rotem Gesicht
Wie ene erschrockene Braut.
Mit Widerscheinaugen
Bestürzten
Von dem was der Himmel entfacht:
Zu prangend für dich
Eine Hochzeit
Zu ewig für dich
Eine Nacht.

Toward Evening

A quarter turn, one more,
And there you are facing evening.
You are red-faced
Like a frightened bride.
Your reflecting eyes
Dismayed
By what the sky is kindling:
Too ornate
A wedding for you
Too eternal
A night.

Weißnoch

Weißnoch, weißnoch
Den Vogel Unheil,
Seh ihn noch hocken,
Seh ihn noch hüpfen
Im Käfig über dem Bett uns.
Seine Federn wuchsen,
Seine Flügel wurden kräftig.
Auch wie ich ihn auf den Schoß nahm,
Ihn hegte und wiegte,
Gleich einer Taube,
Hielt ich ihn auf dem Schoß.
Wie ich ihn fütterte,
Mit Süßholz zuerst,
Dann mit Herzblut,
Daß er nicht aufflöge,
Geierkahl krächzend,
Weißnoch, weißnoch,
Wie er sich losriß,
Geierkahl krächzend
Die Sonne verschlang.

Can't Forget

Can't forget, can't forget
The bird called Calamity.
Still see it perch,
Still see it skip
In its cage by our bed.
Its feathers lengthened,
Its wings grew strong.
Can't forget holding it,
Cradling it, stroking it,
Like a soft dove
I held it against me.
Can't forget feeding it,
Sweetmeats first,
Heartsblood after,
To foil its ascent
As a baldheaded vulture.
Can't forget, can't forget
How it got loose,
The baldheaded vulture,
And swallowed the sun.

In meinem Weinberg

In meinem Weinberg
Blutet die Rebe
So, als sollte noch einmal
Ein übermäßiger Herbst
Mir die Seiten füllen randüber.
So, als sollte aus all
Meinen ziellosen Schritten
Noch einer hervorgehen,
Der beträte ein inneres Land,
Als sollte aus meiner Stirn
Der kalten gepanzerten
Ausfliegen noch
Ein Vogel Paradies.

In My Vineyard

In my vineyard
The vines are bleeding
As if an overwhelming autumn
Should fill me to overflowing
One more time.
As if from among
My erratic steps
One should break through
Into the interior,
As if my forehead
With its cold armor
Should still let fly
A bird of paradise.

Verdächtiges Ich

Überspringen wir doch uns selbst
Meiden wir diese
Ortschaften ausgediente
Vorderes hinteres Elend
Und den erschütterten Menschen.

Wieviele Schneefälle sind
Die kein Auge sieht
Und Meteore wieviele
Stürzen während wir schlafen.

Besinne verdächtiges Ich
Den Rehschädel an der Wand
Die beinweiße schweigende Maske
Und draußen das flirrende Laub
Das deinen Atem nicht braucht.

Suspect Self

Let's omit ourselves
Avoid these
Worn-out locations
Misery left and right
And the shattered human heart.

How many snowfalls
Are seen by no eye
How many meteors
Plunge through our sleep

Consider, suspect self
The deer's head on the wall
The bone-white silent mask
And the flying leaves outside
Which do not need your breath.

Ohne Ort und Ziel

FÜR KLAUS BENDIXEN

Keinen Ort mehr haben
Kein auszuweisendes Ziel
Nicht greifbarer sein
Als Spiegelbilder der Tauben
Auf der regenroten Terrasse
Als der Klagschrei der Eulen
Im Schwarznadelbaum.
Forttragen nichts
Als leichthin jenes mein Tal
In der offenen Hand.
Aufwachen nachts
Ins Tretrad springen
Meine kreisende Himmelsleiter.
Unten wie oben
Ist Anfang und Ende
Oben wie unten
Schlag ich mich frei.

Drifter

FOR KLAUS BENDIXEN

To have no fixed abode
No valid destination
To be no more substantial
Than the mirror image of pigeons
On the red wet terrace
Than the complaint of the owl
In the black spruce trees.
To bear away nothing more
Than this my valley lightly
Inside my open hand.
To wake in the night
Jump on the treadmill
My circular stairway to heaven.
Bottom and top
Are beginning and end
On top and at bottom
I'll tear myself free.

Zuweilen

Zuweilen schläft auch der Dichter
Der alte Verderber der Feste
Ausgezählt hat er sich selber
Gesunken ins Sterntalergras.
Schnellwachsender Traum überspinnt ihm
Die spähenden Augen
Auf seiner Schreibhand
Begatten sich Schmetterlinge
Seine Sturmvögel plappern wie Spatzen
Das liebliche Immer-schon-da.

At Times

At times the poet nods
The old spoiler of banquets
He lies down in the grass
And collects his fee in stars.
A dream shoots up and grows
Over his watchful eyes
Butterflies couple
On his writing hand
His stormy petrels chirp like sparrows
Their lyrical here-we-are.

Meine Neugier

Meine Neugier, die ausgewanderte, ist zurückgekehrt.
Mit blanken Augen spaziert sie wieder
Auf der Seite des Lebens.
Salve, sagt sie, freundliches Schiefgesicht,
Zweijährige Stimme, unschuldig wie ein Veilchen,
Grünohren, Wangen wie Fischhaut, Tausendschön
Alles begrüßt sie, das Häßliche und das Schöne.

Gerade als hätte ich nicht schon längst genug,
Holt sie mir meinen Teil, meinen Löwenteil,
An dem, was geschieht, aus Häusern, die mich nichts angehen.
Ein Ohr soll ich haben für jeden Untergang
Und Augen für jede Gewalttat.

Die schönste Abendröte kommt dagegen nicht auf,
Die zartesten Gräser sind machtlos.
Wie sehne ich mich nach der Zeit, als sie nichts zu bestimmen
    hatte,
Als ich hintrieb ruhig im Kielwasser des Todes,
In den milchigen Strudeln der Träume.

Vergeblich jag ich sie fort, meine Peinigerin.
Da ist sie wieder, trottet und hüpft,
Streift mich mit ihrem heißen Hündinnenatem.

Vergeblich beklage ich mich.
Was für ein schreckliches Lärmen,
Was für ein Gelauf und Geläute,
Was für eine Stimme, die aus mir selber kommt,
Spottdrosselstimme, und sagt,
Was willst du, du lebst.

My Curiosity

My curiosity, the expatriate, has returned.
Bright-eyed, she can be seen strolling
On this side of life again.
Salve, she says, with her kind, crooked face,
Voice of a two-year-old, innocent as a violet,
Cheeks like fish skin, not yet dry behind the ears,
Ugly or beautiful, she welcomes it all.

As if I hadn't had it up to here,
She goes after my portion, my lion's share
Of whatever happens, in houses that aren't my business.
I am to keep an eye out for every tragedy,
An ear to the ground for every violent act.

The loveliest sunset can't compete,
The most delicate grasses are powerless.
How I long for the time when she had no rights,
When I drifted along in the wake of death
In milky eddies of dreaming.

No use running her off, my tormentor.
She comes right back, trotting and bounding,
Her hot, doggy breath brushing my face.

It does no good to complain.
What a terrible racket,
All that running and ringing,
What a voice coming out of myself,
A mockingbird's voice, which says,
What do you want, you are alive.

59

Auferstehung

Manchmal stehen wir auf
Stehen wir zur Auferstehung auf
Mitten am Tage
Mit unserem lebendigen Haar
Mit unserer atmenden Haut.

Nur das Gewohnte ist um uns.
Keine Fata Morgana von Palmen
Mit weidenden Löwen
Und sanften Wölfen.

Die Weckuhren hören nicht auf zu ticken
Ihre Leuchtzeiger löschen nicht aus.

Und dennoch leicht
Und dennoch unverwundbar
Geordnet in geheimnisvolle Ordnung
Vorweggenommen in ein Haus aus Licht.

Resurrection

Sometimes we arise
Arise for the resurrection
In bright daylight
Our hair alive
Our skins breathing.

Only the usual things surround us.
No mirage of palm trees
With grazing lions
And gentle wolves.

The alarm clocks do not stop ticking
Their luminous hands do not go dark.

And even so we are weightless
Even so invulnerable
Part of the secret order
Already at home in a house of light.

From
EIN WORT WEITER
(1965)

Schiffsweiß

Wer hätte in dieser unserer
Mathematischen Welt
Je ein Ding gesehen, das verwest
Und ein Ding, das wurzelt?
Weiß weißes Weiß
Über kurz oder lang
Werden auch wir mit Ölfarbe angestrichen
Dann altern wir nicht mehr
Wir essen Blancmanger
Die Uhren stehen weiß
Nur daß die Nacht
Aufzieht mit Horden unbekannter Sterne.

The White of Ships

In our mathematical world
Who can still remember
Anything that decays
And anything that takes root?
White whitest white
Sooner or later we too
Will get our coats of oil-base paint
Then we'll stop getting older
We'll eat blancmange
The clocks will say white
Except that the night
Drums up hordes of unknown stars.

Nausikaa

Komm wieder ans Land
Tangüberwachsener
Muschelbestückter
Triefender Fremdling
Du
Noch immer der alte
Voll von Männergeschichten
Fragwürdigen Abenteuern
Lieg mir im grasgrünen Bett
Berühre mit salzigen Fingern
Mein Veilchenauge
Meine Goldregenlocken
Fahr weiter nach Ithaka
In dein Alter in deinen Tod
Sag noch eins
Eh du gehst.

Nausicaa

Come back ashore
Dripping stranger
Coated with seaweed
Armored with shells
You
Still the same
Still full of yarns
Unlikely adventures
Lie in my grass-green bed
Touch with salty fingers
My violet eyes
My forsythia hair
Sail on to Ithaca
Into your age your death
Just one more word
Before you go.

Schafe zur Linken

Zaghaft auszusprechendes Wort Glück
Fahrradglocke
Eben nur angeschlagen
Flüchtigster Vogel genährt von keiner Speise
Und doch
Auffliegend zuweilen
Rot golden herrisch
Eherne Wirklichkeit
Wirklicher als
Das wir tragen das Tränenkleid
Als Hagel und Heuschreckenschwarm
Als das Bild der Sommerrose
Im Eisauge des Winters
Zieht
Zieht
Schafe zur Linken.

Sheep at My Left

Timidly spoken the word happiness
A bicycle bell
Barely sounded
A wild bird nourished on nothing
Which nevertheless
Flies up at times
Red gold imperious
Brazen reality
More real than
The garment of tears we wear
Than hail and hordes of locusts
Than the dream of the rose
In the icy eye of winter
Stroll on
Stroll on
Sheep at my left.

Nicht gesagt

Nicht gesagt
Was von der Sonne zu sagen gewesen wäre
Und vom Blitz nicht das einzig richtige
Geschweige denn von der Liebe.

Versuche. Gesuche. Mißlungen
Ungenaue Beschreibung

Weggelassen das Morgenrot
Nicht gesprochen vom Sämann
Und nur am Rande vermerkt
Den Hahnenfuß und das Veilchen.

Euch nicht den Rücken gestärkt
Mit ewiger Seligkeit
Den Verfall nicht geleugnet
Und nicht die Verzweiflung

Den Teufel nicht an die Wand
Weil ich nicht an ihn glaube
Gott nicht gelobt
Aber wer bin ich daß

Left Unsaid

Left unsaid
What should have been said of the sun
And the only word that is right for lightning
Not to mention love.

Gropings. Searches. Misses.
Inexact description.

Sunrise passed over
The plowman omitted
Buttercup and violet
Only in the margin.

No one propped up
With promises of the afterlife
No secret made of decay
And desperation

No images of the devil
Because I don't believe in him
No praises of God
But who am I to

From
KEIN ZAUBERSPRUCH
(1972)

Vögel

Ein Paar Vögel noch immer
Aber wie ungleich jetzt
Einer gierig aufpickend
Den kleinen Lebensrest
Im warmen Laub
Der andere entflogen
Sein klarer Schatten
Gleitet übers Schneefeld
Zieht Kreise drei
Jeder ein wenig blasser
Kein Schrei aus den Wolken
Keine Feder herab.

Birds

Still here, a pair of birds
So unalike now
One pecking greedily
At the speck of leftover life
In the warm leaves
The other flown
Its clear shadow
Glides over the field of snow
Makes three circles
Each a little paler
No cry from the clouds
No feather descending.

Die Gärten

Die Gärten untergepflügt
Die Wälder zermahlen
Auf dem Nacktfels die Hütte gebaut
Umzäunt mit geschütteten Steinen
Eine Cactusfeige gesetzt
Einen Brunnen gegraben
Mich selbst
Ans Drehkreuz gespannt
Da geh ich geh ich rundum
Schöpfe mein brackiges Lebenswasser
Schreie den Eselsschrei
Hinauf zu den Sternen.

The Gardens

The gardens plowed under
The forests crushed
My shack built on bare rock
Its fence a heap of stones
The cactus fig planted
The well dug
Myself
Harnessed to the cart
Going around around
Drawing the brackish water of my life
Braying the donkey's bray
In the direction of the stars.

Erste Hilfe

Wo immer du
Du warst nicht unerreichbar
Meine Gierhand riß dich zurück
Aus dem schmutzigen Meersaum
Im Rundnetz
Über den Strand zu den Felsen
Zog ich dich Riese.
Wie schienst du mir unzerstört
Ich wärmte deinen Leib mit meinem Leibe
Meinen Atem stieß ich dir in den Mund
Nur daß deine Augen unter dem roten Garn
Die schon erstarrten hart wie Kieselsteine
Nichts spiegelten
Nicht den Himmel
Noch meine zornigen Tränen.

First Aid

Wherever you were
You were never out of reach
My greedy hands pulled you back
In the round net
From the dirty rim of the sea
I dragged you, giant
Across the beach to the cliffs
How unravaged you seemed to me
I warmed your body with mine
Forced my breath in your mouth
O but your eyes under the red yarn
Already fixed and hard as gravel
Mirrored nothing
Not the sky
Nor my angry tears.

Dies immer noch

Dies: immer noch wollen
Den Laden
Immer noch aufziehen wollen
Das Hinterhaus
Immer noch auf die Netzhaut
Und das Siebenuhrmorgenzimmer

Immer noch ausgehen wollen
Die altbackene Straße hinunter
Entlang den Fenstern
Voll vergeblicher Hilfeschreie
Und einsammeln im Drahtkorb
Schicksal um Schicksal

Auf der Zunge das alte Ungereimte
Mein Schritt eine Uhr die abläuft
In der Hand noch immer
Das Pappfähnchen Zuversicht
Hinter mir keine Armee
Dann und wann Kinder.

Still Game

Still game for this:
To pull up
The window shades and discover
The house in back
Still fixed on the retina
And this room at seven a.m.

Still game to go out
Down the old cobbled street
Passing windows
Crowded with futile cries for help
And collecting fate
After fate in my wire basket

The same old gibberish on my tongue
My steps a clock running down
My hand still clutching
The paper pennant of confidence
No army behind me
Now and then children.

Mein Land

Ich habe mein Land abgesteckt
Mit gefrorenen Fischen
Und mit raschelndem Maiskolbenlaub
Meinen Weg ins Freie
Eisfarren zieh ich mir auf
An meiner Fensterscheibe
Für meine Besucher
Hauch ich ein kreisrundes Loch
Sie sehen meine Augen
Meine vergeblich
Winkenden Wimpern
Um Mitternacht fegt durch den Mais
Der Slalom der Geister.

My Ground

I have staked out my ground
With frozen fishes
My path to freedom
Is marked by rustling corn husks
I raise ice ferns
On my windowpane
I breathe a circular hole
For my visitors
They see my eyes
My lashes waving
In vain
Around midnight the slalom of ghosts
Sweeps through the corn.

Frauenfunk

Eines Tages sprech ich im Rundfunk
Gegen Morgen wenn niemand mehr zuhört
Meine gewissen Rezepte

Gießt Milch ins Telefon
Laßt Katzen hecken
In der Geschirrspülmaschine
Zerstampft die Uhren im Waschtrog
Tretet aus Euren Schuhen

Würzt den Pfirsich mit Paprika
Und das Beinfleisch mit Honig

Lehrt eure Kinder das Füchsinneneinmaleins
Dreht die Blätter im Garten auf ihre Silberseite
Beredet euch mit dem Kauz

Wenn es Sommer wird zieht euren Pelz an
Trefft die aus den Bergen kommen
Die Dudelsackpfeifer
Tretet aus Euren Schuhen

Seid nicht so sicher
Daß es Abend wird
Nicht so sicher
Daß Gott euch liebt.

Broadcast for Women

I give a talk on the radio
Toward morning when no one is listening
I offer my recipes

Pour milk into the telephone
Let your cats sleep
In the dishwashers
Smash the clocks in your washing machines
Leave your shoes behind

Season your peaches with paprika
And your soup meat with honey

Teach your children the alphabet of foxes
Turn the leaves in your gardens silver side up
Take the advice of the owl

When summer arrives put on your furs
Go meet the ones with the bagpipes
Who come from inside the mountains
Leave your shoes behind

Don't be too sure
Evening will come
Don't be too sure
That God loves you.

Klingelfahrer

Kommt jetzt ihr Engel
Ihr Klingelfahrer
Verkleidet als Prüfer
Von Rentenpapieren
Oder als bärtige Händler
Mir Teppiche beduinisch
Unter die Füße zu breiten
Rosen auf schwarzem Grund
Naht euch zigeunerisch
Lest mir aus der Hand von den Lippen
Die alte zweideutige Wahrheit
Verkauft mir die Stimme der Amsel
Und das siebenversiegelte Buch
Klagt stellt euch bedürftig
Ich weiß
Ich erkenne euch hinter den Masken
Schon geh ich und leere den Spartopf
Mit sanftem Finger
Brecht ihr mir das Genick.

Peddlers Ringing Bells

Come to me angels
Peddlers ringing bells
Disguised as inspectors
Of old age pensions
Or bearded merchants
Bedouins spreading
Rugs underfoot
Roses on a black ground
Come to me like the gypsies
Read from my palm my lips
The old ambiguous truth
Sell me the voice of the blackbird
And the book with the seven seals
Complain say you are needy
I know
I recognize you behind your masks
Already I empty the piggy bank
With gentle fingers
You break my neck.

Meine Schwester Lonja

Dein Leben war wie es sein soll.
Kein Fisch
Ging dir ins Netz
Wenn du liebtest fandest du nicht
Die richtigen Worte
Niemand entlohnte dich nach deinem Verdienst.

Verschwenderisch Unerschrockene
Dein Mund voller Verse
Schrie nach Gerechtigkeit
Machte kein Zugeständnis.

Es gibt eine Ungunst der Sterne
Die edler ist als die Glückszahl
Eine heilige Unvernunft
Die fliegt uns vorüber kometisch
Genügt nicht
Ist mehr als genug.

My Sister Lonja

Your life was as it should be.
No fish
Landed in your net
In love you could not find
The right words
No one paid you what you were worth.

Fearless prodigal
Your mouth full of poems
Cried out for justice
Made no concessions.

There is an ill will in the stars
More sublime than a lucky number
A holy unreason which flies
Past us like a comet
Not enough
More than enough.

Der Heizer

Rückkehr immer wieder
Nach dem Hinausgeschossen-
Werden ins All
Wo ich irrte unbefugt
Ausgestattet nicht mit den Ewigkeitsaugen
Mit den feinen Fühlhörnern der Seelen

Wo ich torkelte grober Fremdling
Der die Milchstraßennetze zerreißt
Den man zurückstürzt endlich auf sein Bett
In sein stickiges Fleisch und Blut

Unwilling dämmert der Novembermorgen
Die Röhren auf und ab
Geht mit Steigeisenfüßen
Der Heizer.

The Stoker

Always the return
After being shot
Into space
Where I wandered unauthorized
Not equipped with the eyes of eternity
With the delicate feelers of souls

Where I bumbled a crude stranger
Tearing the nets of the Milky Way
To be thrown back on my bed
Into my stuffy flesh and blood

Dawn comes reluctantly this November
Up and down the pipes
The stoker
Is climbing on spiked feet.

Kein Zauberspruch

Einiges wäre
Entgegenzuhalten
Der jungen vom Sturm
Geköpften Schwarznuß
Und allen viel schrecklicheren
Gorgonenhäuptern

Kein Zauberspruch
Keine Geste
Worte einmal aufgeschrieben
Will ich meinem
Text einfügen

Etwa diese
Aus Aquino
Weil das Böse ist
Ist Gott.

No Magic Formula

Some answers are possible
In the face of
The storm-uprooted young
Black walnut sapling
And all the other
More frightful heads of the Gorgon

No magic formula
No ritual gesture
Words written a long time ago
Are what I enter
Into my text

Such as these
From Aquinas
Because evil exists
God exists.

Am Feiertag

Als die Osterglocken läuteten
Mit den Tönen h e g fis
War ich siebzig Jahre und siebzig Tage alt
Ich hatte erfahren
Daß siebzig Jahre ein Loch sind
In das einer fällt
Und sich rettet an schlüpfrigen Wänden

An Ostern war ich so weit
Daß ich hoch oben
Die kleine Sternmagnolie sehen konnte
Und wie der Wind ihr die Blüten zerriß

Im Fernsehen wurde der Attentäter gezeigt
Der Gärtner Sein rundes törichtes Gesicht
Und sein feststehendes Messer
In Hottes Wolfsschanze
Einer Kneipe in Berlin
Legen sie wieder die alten Platten auf
Vor allem diese: Preußens Gloria

In San Giovanni im Lateran
Sah ich die Kerzen alle zurückgekehrt
Die schwarzen Banner der Trauer rot überhangen
Die hölzernen Ratschen
Gaben ihr unterweltliches Knarren auf
Auch die Ungläubigen atmeten freier

Als die Osterglocken läuteten
Hatten auf der Straße
Schon ein paar hundert Autofahrer
Ihren Geist aufgegeben
Das große Schlachten
Wie wenn am Feiertag
Hatte begonnen

94

Holiday

When the Easter bells rang
B E G F-sharp
I was seventy years and seventy days old
I had discovered
That seventy years are a hole
You fall into
And climb out of up slippery walls

By Easter I had made it
To where I could see the small
Star magnolia above my head
And how the wind was tearing its blossoms

On television they showed the killer
A gardener His round foolish face
And his protruding knife
In a tavern in Berlin
Called Hottes Wolfsschanze
They are going back to the old records
Especially this one: Glorious Prussia

In San Giovanni Lateran
I saw the candles which had returned
The black banners of mourning covered with red
The wooden kneelers
Gave up their purgatorial creaking
Even the unbelievers breathed easier

When the Easter bells rang
Several hundred motorists
Had already
Given up the ghost
The great
Holiday slaughter
Had begun

95

Heuer wurden zur Osterzeit
In einigen Städten
Mondsteine herumgereicht
Authentisches aus dem Astronautengcpäck
Nichts Besonderes
Einfach Geröll

Le fond de l'air est froid
Sagte meine Mutter
Die noch französisch erzogen worden war
Le fond de l'air . . .

Diese ärmlichen Vorfrühlingsfreuden
Weidenschleier
Und Eidottergelbes
Dahinter die häßlichen Häuser
Und Auferstehung.
Das Wort
Auferstehung.

In some cities
This year around Easter
Moon rocks were on display
Authentic stuff from the astronauts' gear
Nothing much
Plain rubble

Le fond de l'air est froid
My mother used to say
Who was still raised on French
Le fond de l'air . . .

These meager pleasures of not-yet-spring
Willow lace
And yellow the color of egg yolk
In front of the ugly houses
And resurrection
The word
Resurrection.

Zumutungen

Immer mir vor den Augen
Diese verwandelte Stadt
Die blühte brannte und in Asche fiel
Und wieder blühte
Wenn man das
So nennen kann
Diese Hochhäuser Schreibstubentürme
Nachts mit erloschenen Augen
Da wohn ich
Im Zahlengeflüster
Und verstehe von Zahlen nichts
Und bleibe
Aus Trägheit oder
Aus Treue.

Und draußen wieder die Flucht
Jenes steile
Bachufer hinunter
Mit Klumpfüßen aus Lehm
Maschinengewehr-
Geprassel im Rücken
Und die Stirn gedrückt
In die kränklichen Anemonen.

Und immer wieder der Ruf
Dieses einzige Wort NEIN
Mit dem jemand sich aufbäumt
Gegen weiß Gott welche schreckliche Zumutung.

Ein Geräusch was hat so geklungen
Die nebelpelzige Traube
Die abgeschnitten in den Eimer fiel

Injunctions

Always before my eyes
This altered city
Which blossomed burned and fell into ashes
And blossomed again
If you can
Call it that
These high-rises office-towers
With snuffed-out eyes at night
I live here
Amidst whispering numbers
Not knowing anything about numbers
And stay
Out of laziness or
Out of loyalty.

And outside the flight repeats itself
Club-footed with mud
Down the steep
River embankment
The rattle of machine guns
Close at my back
And my face pressed
Into the sickly anemones.

And over and over the cry
The single word NO
Which is someone's way of rising
Against God knows what terrible injunction.

A noise what was it sounded like that
The cut-down grapes
Furred and misty hitting the pails

Und so
Klirrte der Eimer in die Bütte geleert
Und so
Stampften die schweren Schritte der Büttenträger
Den Hang hinab.

O mein funkelndes Märzlicht im Osten
Klirrend abfallende Zapfen
Und die Vögel zahllose über der Niederung
Pferde im groben Winterhaar
Ohne Sattel und Zaum.

Meine Schwester schloß ihre Briefe an mich mit den Worten
Hähnchen und Hühnchen gingen auf den Nußberg
Oder mit dieser Zeile geheimnisvoll
Rotkehlchen Liebseelchen.

Unsere Väter wir erfuhren es noch
Waren unruhig und ernst.
Der eine einzige, der lachen konnte
Nahm sich das Leben.

Der Eisläufer setzte an
Zum Doppelsalchow
Wirbelte sich in die Luft
Kam zu Boden ohne Erschütterung
Und schwingt schon weiter
Leicht wie ein Gedanke
Und fliegt
Und fliegt.

And this is how
The pails clanked when they tipped and emptied
And this is how
The heavy feet of the basket-bearers
Tramped down the hill.

O my glittering eastern March light
Falling icicles clanking
And countless birds above the lowland
Horses in their rough winter coats
Without saddle or bridle.

My sister's letters used to close with the words
Jack and Jill went up the hill
Or with the secret code
Star-light star-bright.

We could see our fathers
Were worried and glum.
The only one who was able to laugh
Took his own life.

The skater got ready
For the double Salchow
Whirled around in the air
Landed on the ice without a thud
And goes on dancing
As easily as a thought
And flies
And is flying.

Wer hätte das gedacht

Ein Dichter hat in einem Heft
Altpruzzische Vokabeln aufgeschrieben
In seinem Zimmer hat ein Bild gehangen
Ein Wolf in öder Schneelandschaft
Entsetzlich einsam
Er hat in diesem Zimmer auch
Ein Klavichord gehabt
Und einige Ikonen
Auch eine Sammlung
Handgeschriebener Lieder
Litauen in Berlin
Als er tot war
Hat jemand
Dieses Zimmer beschrieben
Sehr genau
Auch photographiert
In memoriam

In einigen Jahrzehnten
Kommen wir auf die Welt
Immer noch zwischen den Beinen einer Frau
Aber vorgeburtlich geplant
So daß wir gleich alles können
Ohne Übung
Wie der Zeichner Aubrey Beardsley
Bei dem jeder Strich von Anfang an saß
Und der bei seinem jungen Tod
Nur Meisterwerke hinterließ.

Wer hätte das gedacht
Nach den Schlägern und Rockern

Who Would Have Thought It

A poet put Old Prussian*
Words into his notebook
A picture hung in his room
A wolf in a wilderness of snow
Unbearably lonely
He had a clavichord
In this same room
Also several icons
And a collection
Of handwritten songs
Lithuania in Berlin
When he was dead
Someone
Described this room
In great detail
And took photographs
In memoriam

In a few decades
We will enter the world
Still between the legs of women
But so well designed
That we'll know how to do everything
Without any training
Like Aubrey Beardsley
Who never erased a line
And left only masterpieces
When he died young

Who would have thought it
After the black leather jackets

* The now extinct language of the early Lithuanians

Die Kinder Gottes
Ihr sanftes Gurren
Jesus
Jesus

Was macht ihr mit eurer Zeit?
Danke wir kommen zurecht
Wir vertreiben sie
Schlagen sie tot
Nur die Tage der Alten
Mit ihren unauffindbaren Worten
Entgleitenden Dingen
Sind ein gelassenes Lächeln
Auf keinem grünen Zweig

Seht die Hallen gerüstet die Becken
Funktürme aufgezogen
Stahlnetze geworfen
Schnellstraßen geglättet
Auch unter der Erde
Mastochsen eingefroren
Bierfässer gestapelt
Zehntausende, alles
Für diese vielleicht letzten Spiele
Und das andere ferne Olympia
Unter die Pinienkronen
Gesunken
Still

Einer träumte der Kopf
Sei ihm abgeschlagen

The children of God
Cooing
Jesus
Jesus

How do you spend your time?
Thank you we manage
We waste it
Kill it
Only the days of the old
With their missing words
Escaping things
Are placid, a smile
With no place to go

Look here: stadiums pools
Antennas mounted
Steel nets in place
Expressways smoothed
Even underground
Prime beef frozen
Barrels of beer stacked high
Tens of thousands, all
For these Games which may be the last
And that other distant Olympia
Sunk
Beneath the pines
Silent

Someone dreamed that his head
Had been cut off

Säße nur lose noch auf
Er stützte ihn unter dem Blutring
Mit beiden Händen
Vorsichtig ging er die steinerne Treppe hinab
Er fürchtete, sagte er, sehr
Eine Gehirnerschütterung zu bekommen
Wenn er ihm entglitte der Kopf
Und hüpfte die Stufen.

And rested loosely on his neck
He steadied it with both hands
Below the bloodline
He was careful walking down the stone stairs
Afraid, he said, he might suffer
A brain concussion
If his head should slip
And bounce on the steps.

Abschied von Rom

Wo man hinaufging
Unter Platanen
Die schräge Straße
Zur Villa Medici
Mit Wasserschleiern
Über Stirn und Wangen
Und Tropfen hergeschleudert
Judasbaum

Orte mir lange bekannte
Sterben ab
Während du auftauchst
Australisches Sydney
Mit den Betonsegeln schlohweißen
Deiner Hafenoper
Und weiter landeinwärts
Dem undurchdringlichen Busch

Die einen Meeressaum
Zur Heimat haben
Ungaretti Montale Quasimodo
Sind gut daran
Alles lesen sie auf
Vor der eigenen Tür
Und finden als Strandgut
Täglich die Ewigkeit

Farewell to Rome

Where we climbed toward
The Villa Medici
A slanting street
Beneath plane trees
Veils of water
On cheeks and foreheads
Drops hurled at us
Judas tree

Long-familiar places
Are dying out
While you arise
Australian Sydney
With sails of white concrete
Your opera house in the harbor
And in the interior
Your impenetrable bush

How lucky they are
Ungaretti Montale Quasimodo
Who make their home
At the edge of the sea
They pick up the world
In front of their doors
Each day they discover eternity
Washed up on the beach

O meine Gedankenwege
Springböckig steppenüber
Flutend in Wellen
Nicht wie auf dem kalten Bildschirm
Vielmehr ich bin's
Mein Schweiß auf der Haut
Mein Brennen in der Kehle
Meine Dornen im Fuß.

Als James Ensor
Seinen Gekreuzigten malte
Und die Tafel zu seinen Häupten
Schrieb er auf die Tafel
Nicht INRI
Ensor.

O the moves of my mind
A springbok on the plains
Flotsam in oceans
Not images on the cold screen
But me
My skin sweating
My throat burning
My feet pierced by thorns

When James Ensor
Painted the crucifixion
And the tablet at the head
He wrote on the tablet
Not INRI
Ensor.

THE LOCKERT LIBRARY OF POETRY
IN TRANSLATION

Library of Congress Cataloging in Publication Data

Kaschnitz, Marie Luise, 1901-1974.
    Selected later poems of Marie Luise Kaschnitz.

    (The Lockert library of poetry in translation)
    I. Mueller, Lisel.   II. Title.
PT2621.A73A26   831'.912   80-7537
ISBN 0-691-06442-3
ISBN 0-691-01374-8 (pbk.)